THE ROOTS OF HUMANITY

BY JIM OLLHOFF

Published by ABDO Publishing Company, 8000 West 78th Street, Suite 310, Edina, MN 55439. Copyright ©2011 by Abdo Consulting Group, Inc. International copyrights reserved in all countries. No part of this book may be reproduced in any form without written permission from the publisher. ABDO & Daughters™ is a trademark and logo of ABDO Publishing Company.

Printed in the United States of America, North Mankato, Minnesota.
112010
012011

 PRINTED ON RECYCLED PAPER

Editor: John Hamilton

Graphic Design: John Hamilton

Cover Design: Neil Klinepier

Cover Photo: Getty Images

Interior Photos and Illustrations: Getty Images-pgs 11, 15, 16-17, 18-19, 20, 23, 24-25, 28-29; Granger Collection-pgs 22, 26, 27; John Hamilton-p. 21; iStockphoto-pgs 4-5, 8-9; Montana Historical Society-p. 21; Photo Researchers-p. 10, 12-13; ThinkStock-pgs 6, 7, 14.

Library of Congress Cataloging-in-Publication Data

Ollhoff, Jim, 1959-
  The roots of humanity / Jim Ollhoff.
     p. cm. -- (African-American history)
  Includes index.
  ISBN 978-1-61714-713-5
  1. Black race--Juvenile literature. 2. Race--Juvenile literature. 3. Human skin color--Juvenile literature. 4. Africa--Juvenile literature. 5. African Americans--History--Juvenile literature. 6. Racism--Juvenile literature. I. Title. II. Series.

HT1581.O55 2011
305.896--dc22

                                                    2010038368

CONTENTS

What's in a Name? 4

Skin Color 8

The Roots of Humanity...12

Africa the Continent..14

African History 16

Bringing Africa With Them 20

Early Views on Race 24

The Development of Racism 28

Glossary...30

Index 32

WHAT'S IN A NAME?

What do we call people who have skin that is one color or another?
There is no perfect word that describes people of African descent, since words have meanings that change over time. In fact, there is no perfect word to describe anyone's skin color.

When the Spanish and Portuguese landed in Africa in the 1400s, they called the people there "negro," which is the Spanish word for "black." This was a popular term through the early 1900s, but it fell into disuse.

Today, it is not only considered an old-fashioned word, some people think it is offensive. The word "negro" became offensive because it reminded people of the horrors of slavery.

Another term that became popular in the 1800s was "colored." It was a common term until the 1950s. Just like the term negro, it eventually became an offensive name also. In the 1960s, people began to use the term "Afro-American." It also fell into disuse.

How about the term "black"? It is a common term today, but it isn't perfect either. Australian Aborigines have skin color that is as black as people of African descent. So do many others, including the Maori of New Zealand, many people in the Philippines, and people from the area of Madras, India.

Another common term is African American. It isn't perfect either, since there are many different skin colors that are represented across the continent of Africa.

Even the term "of African descent" has problems. Because humanity began in Africa hundreds of thousands of years ago, every person living on Earth today is of African descent.

No term referring to any kind of skin color is perfect. Words and their meanings change as the years go by. For most people of recent African descent living in North America, "black" and "African American" are the most common terms used today.

Using words to describe traits such as skin color can lead to racist attitudes.

For most people of African descent living in North America today, the most common terms used are "black" and "African American."

SKIN COLOR

Since the first civilizations, people have been trying to figure out why people have different skin color. Scientists in the 1700s and 1800s had a lot of different ideas about skin color.

Some scientists said that skin changed color in climates with different temperature. Some said skin color varied because of the food people ate. Others said it was the elevation of the land. Some said different behaviors and customs around the world caused people's skin to change color. Probably the most common view was that God created different "races" of people at different times.

Today, we know that skin color is caused by melanin, a compound in the cells of the skin. The more melanin people have, the darker they are. Melanin protects people from the harmful rays of the sun. So, when the entire human population lived in Africa 100,000 years ago, everyone was black. The high amount of melanin kept people from developing skin cancer, a disease caused by too much sunlight. Today, skin cancer is not very common among black people.

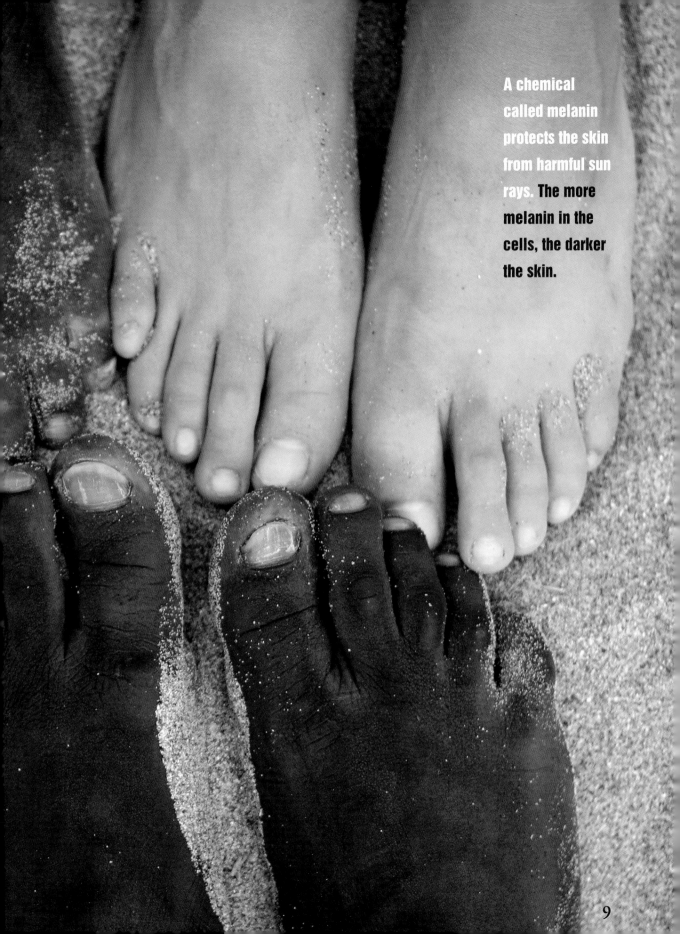

A chemical called melanin protects the skin from harmful sun rays. The more melanin in the cells, the darker the skin.

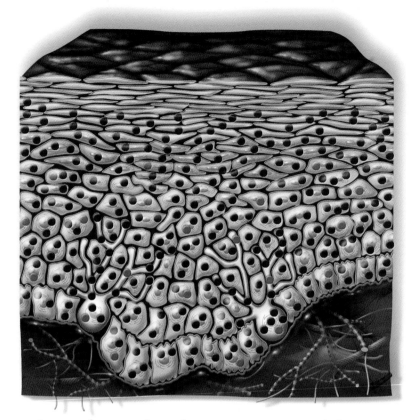

A cross-section of human skin showing high concentrations of melanin (brown dots within the skin cells). Melanin protects the skin against the harmful rays of the sun.

As people moved north into Europe and Asia, they were in shelters more often because of the cold weather. They didn't need as much melanin. In fact, their skin needed a way to absorb more sunlight, because the body transforms sunlight into vitamin D. The more melanin a person's skin has, the less vitamin D they absorb in a given time period. In northern climates, people were inside a lot of the time, so they needed less melanin—lighter skin—in order to get enough vitamin D during the times they were in the sun.

They didn't need as much melanin, since they didn't need as much protection from skin cancer. In the high latitudes, over the centuries, skin became lighter colored. The lightest skin could be found in the highest latitudes—in countries like Scotland, Finland, and Sweden.

Humans evolved with different skin colors in order to live in different places on Earth. We know that "race," as scientists in the 1700s understood it, does not really exist. There is only one human species, and our bodies have evolved to live in different places.

THE ROOTS OF HUMANITY

According to the scientists who study evolution, the eastern side of Africa seems to be the birthplace of humanity. The first modern humans appeared at least 100,000 years ago, and possibly much earlier. There are many different kinds of hominids, or two-legged primates.

Evolutionary scientists don't always agree on how the family tree looks. There are still more questions than answers about how humans evolved. Some scientists say the earliest human ancestor was born six million years ago. However, it is difficult to make concrete statements about events that happened that long ago. There is little evidence, such as skeletons, left to examine.

The first human-like hominid was probably Homo erectus, who emerged about 1.8 million years ago. These hominids used tools, lived in family groups, and hunted. Many left Africa and lived in the Middle East and Asia. There were at least a dozen different hominid species before modern humans, now all extinct.

About 100,000 years ago, Homo sapiens, modern humans, emerged in Africa. About 60,000 or 70,000 years ago, some people left Africa and traveled east to Asia. Later, other groups traveled to the Middle East and Europe. Other Homo sapiens stayed in Africa, moving into various parts of the continent.

A family of Homo erectus hominids preparing meat after a successful hunting expedition.

AFRICA THE
CONTINENT

Africa is the second-largest continent in the world (the largest is Asia). Africa takes up more than 20 percent of the Earth's land area. Today, more than 50 countries make up Africa. More than 1,000 languages are spoken, and the continent is home to almost one billion people.

Africa is often divided into five geographic areas: north, east, west, middle, and south. Northern Africa is a hot desert area. Arabic and French speakers inhabit the countries to the north. The Sahara Desert is one of the most visible parts of northern Africa's geography. It stretches across the continent, and is the largest hot desert in the world.

Eastern Africa has a population of both Christians and Muslims, and includes countries such as Kenya and Tanzania. Western Africa also has a Christian and Muslim mix, and includes countries like Mali and Nigeria. Middle Africa has large areas of jungle, and includes the countries of Angola and the Democratic Republic of the Congo. Southern Africa includes the country of South Africa, a large tourism center and important energy producer.

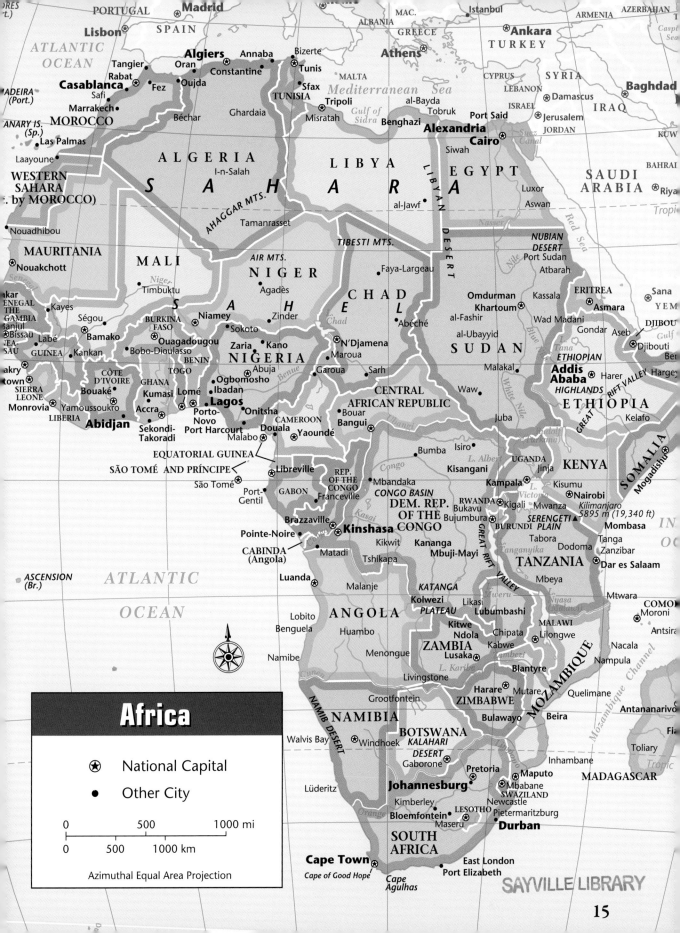

Africa

★ National Capital
● Other City

0   500   1000 mi

0   500   1000 km

Azimuthal Equal Area Projection

AFRICAN
HISTORY

Modern humans appeared in Africa about 100,000 years ago. They ate wild plants and hunted, living in family groups and moving wherever there was food. About 6000 BC, the climate grew warmer. The Sahara Desert got bigger, and it became more difficult to follow food sources. So, people began to plant crops. As farming increased, the population grew, and so kingdoms began to grow.

The first kingdom to grow was in Egypt. But other kingdoms, both large and small, began to spring up. Empires in Africa began to trade with empires in western Asia and the Middle East. In about 800 BC, the Phoenicians, a people from the Middle East, founded the city of Carthage in northern Africa. The Romans and the Carthaginians had many epic battles.

Around 650 AD, Islam spread into northern and western Africa. By 900 AD, people in western Africa were trading slaves, gold, and salt to other parts of the continent, plus areas as far away as China.

The pyramids of Giza, Egypt.

When Portuguese explorers and traders arrived in western Africa in the mid-1400s, they found three main kingdoms: Ghana, Mali, and Songhai. The Portuguese, like other European countries, were interested in finding treasure—and Africa had plenty of treasure. Europeans had more advanced weapons technology, and used it to take whatever they wanted. Gold was a major find for the Europeans, but before long, slavery became a very profitable industry.

In the late 1800s, European countries continued to take treasure out of Africa. They needed raw materials for their factories, and Africa was their source of choice.

The Europeans believed that since their weapons were technologically superior, they had the right to take whatever they wanted.

Several European countries claimed ownership of many parts of Africa. They created colonies that were under the control of the Europeans. Most African countries finally became independent from European countries in the 1950s and 1960s.

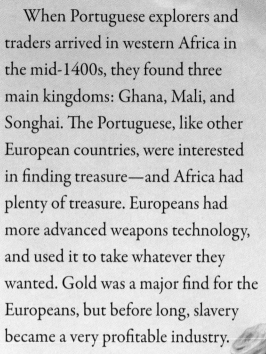

The Slave Trade, an engraving by J.R. Smith, shows English slave traders at work. African family members were often separated when they were sold into slavery.

BRINGING AFRICA WITH THEM

In the 1600s, slave traders found a market for slaves in what would later become the United States. The Africans who were kidnapped and brought to North America tried to bring parts of their culture with them. This was difficult because slave owners often tried to get slaves from different areas of Africa. This meant that many slaves didn't understand each other, since they spoke different languages. Slave owners thought this would make it harder for them to plan an escape or revolt.

In Africa, people sang together as they worked in the fields. It helped them pass the time, but it also strengthened community bonds. This is one of the customs Africans brought to America.

Slaves picking cotton on a Southern plantation.

Lewis and Clark at Three Forks, a painting by E.S. Paxson. York is holding a rifle, second from left.

York (1770?–1832?)

When Meriwether Lewis and William Clark were asked by President Thomas Jefferson to explore the western part of the North American continent, Clark's slave, York, also joined the expedition. The Lewis and Clark Expedition made its way to the Pacific Ocean and back in 1804–1806, when few white people had seen anything west of the Mississippi River.

Even though York was a slave, he participated as a full member of the expedition. He voted with everyone else. He carried a rifle at a time when slaves were not allowed to carry weapons. He was especially skilled at hunting and scouting.

In 1811, several years after the expedition, William Clark granted York his freedom. York started a freighting business in Tennessee and Kentucky. He probably died of cholera sometime in 1832.

A bronze sculpture by Bob Scrivner, which stands in Great Falls, Montana. From left to right: York, Meriwether Lewis, and William Clark.

Br'er Rabbit and Br'er Possum. Br'er Rabbit was a figure in African mythology, who later became a character in popular African American folktales.

People brought some African religions with them, such as the western African religion of Vodun, which emphasizes spirits and ancestor worship. Slave owners sometimes required slaves to practice Catholicism, and so many slaves blended their native religion with Catholicism.

Certain stories from the mythology of Africa were also brought to the New World. One popular figure in African mythology is the rabbit, a clever trickster. The mythology evolved into stories of Brother Rabbit, or Br'er Rabbit, and continued to be passed down to black Americans.

"Imagination! who can sing thy force? Or who describe the swiftness of thy course?"—Phillis Wheatley, excerpt from *On Imagination*

In 1773, Phillis Wheatley published a book entitled Poems on Various Subjects, Religious and Moral.

Phillis Wheatley (1753–1784)

Born in Senegal, Africa, Phillis Wheatley was kidnapped at the age of seven or eight. She was put on a slave ship called the *Phillis*, which is where she got her first name. When the ship reached the American colonies, she was purchased by John and Susannah Wheatley of Massachusetts.

Susannah Wheatley taught Phillis how to read and write. From a very young age, Phillis became a lover of words. She read all the books she could find, and began to compose beautiful poetry. She became a sensation in England and the United States. She was possibly the most famous African American at the time. She died in 1784.

EARLY VIEWS ON RACE

One of the most important early scientists to identify skin color as a race was Carl Linnaeus (1707–1778). He was a Swedish botanist and zoologist. He invented a way to classify plants and animals according to their Latin titles. His classification method is still in use today.

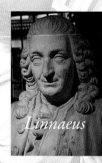

Linnaeus

In 1767, Linnaeus identified five races of people:

• The *Americanus*, which were the Native Americans, or red-skinned people.

• The *Asiaticus*, people from Asia with yellow skin.

• The *Africanus*, the people from Africa with black skin.

• The *Europeanus*, the people from countries in Europe who had white skin.

• The *Monstrosus*, the monster people. In those days, many people believed in human-animal hybrids, such as wolf-people, horse-people, and goat-people.

Within a few years, another influential scientist came along, by the name of Johann Friedrich Blumenbach (1752–1840). A German doctor, he had a slightly different way of looking at  race than Linnaeus. Blumenbach made measurements of many different skulls, calling his study "craniometrical research." This made his method of classifying people sound very scientific. He classified all humans into one of five races:

- Caucasian, or white-skinned;
- Malayan, or brown-skinned;
- Mongolian, or yellow-skinned;
- Negroid, or black-skinned;
- American, or red-skinned.

Blumenbach decided that skull measurements and skin color were related to personality. He said Caucasians were the most intelligent and most productive (Blumenbach was Caucasian), and that the Negroid race was not intelligent and not productive. Later in life, he said he was wrong, but people remembered his first comments about it. It was a way for Europeans to see themselves in a privileged position. It gave them a reason to treat others poorly.

An illustration of the five types into which German anthropologist Johann Friedrich Blumenbach divided the human race: Caucasian (center), Mongolian, Malayan, Ethiopian, and American (clockwise from top right).

Scientific racism gives people excuses to have prejudices against other groups. These theories sound like hard science, but they are really just ways to justify racist opinions.

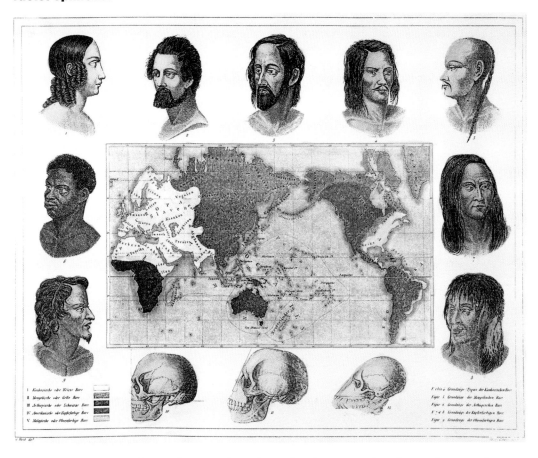

A German study of racial types, based on the theories of anthropologist Johann Friedrich Blumenbach.

Blumenbach's early work was something called "scientific racism." This is when "science" gives some people a reason to have prejudiced ideas about another group. It's actually not science at all, but someone's racist opinion that is cloaked in scientific-sounding words. Scientific racism became a common way for one group to justify treating other groups badly. In fact, many of these kinds of "scientific racist" ideas became a way to justify slavery.

THE DEVELOPMENT OF RACISM

Racism is when someone says an individual has certain qualities because they have a particular skin color or other physical trait. Racism is the belief that people of one skin color are better than people of another skin color. While there has probably always been racism, it became the central issue in the slave trade. Slave traders and owners justified their actions because they believed they were better than the Africans used as slaves.

Racism can exist without slavery. Racism still exists today. It is usually motivated by power and fear. Racists are afraid of "those people," and want to have power over "them." Rather than seeing everyone as people who deserve respect, racists believe "those people" don't deserve respect.

Slavery has existed since civilization began. However, slavery was almost always based on prisoners-of-war. So, if one kingdom conquered another kingdom, people from the conquered kingdom often became slaves. The idea of slavery based on skin color was an idea that began in the 1500s as Europeans captured Africans. The racist ideas of slavery based on skin color were horribly expanded in the United States, beginning in the 1600s.

People simulate a slavery scene in Abidjan, Ivory Coast, as part of the celebrations to mark the 50th anniversary of the Independence of Ivory Coast on August 7, 1960.

GLOSSARY

COLONY

COLONY

A place, usually occupied by settlers, that is under the control of another country. Colonies were often created to benefit the mother country, usually by sending back needed raw materials such as crops, minerals, or lumber.

EVOLUTION

The theory that living creatures change and adapt to the changes in their environment. Early people lived in eastern Africa, which gets a lot of sunlight. Early people's skin contained much melanin, a chemical that darkened the skin to protect it from harmful rays from the sun. When people started migrating out of Africa to lands in the north, cold weather forced them indoors much of the year, so they weren't exposed to the sun as much. The forces of evolution caused people's skin color to lighten, which made it easier for their bodies to convert the sun's rays to vitamin D, which is needed for building strong bones.

HOMINID

A two-legged primate that walks upright. Modern humans are hominids.

HOMO ERECTUS

The first human-like hominids, who emerged about 1.8 million years ago in eastern Africa.

Homo sapiens

Homo sapiens are modern humans. They first emerged about 100,000 years ago in Africa.

Melanin

A compound found in the cells of human skin that causes skin coloration. More melanin causes darker skin, and provides protection against harmful rays of the sun.

New World

After the early expeditions of European explorers, North and South America were referred to as the New World.

Racism

The belief that people of one skin color are better than a people of another skin color; or, that individuals of a certain skin color have certain characteristics *because* of their skin color.

Scientific Racism

A racist opinion that is cloaked in scientific-sounding words.

Vitamin D

A vitamin that is produced in the skin after exposure to ultraviolet light from the sun. Vitamin D promotes strong bones.

Vodun

A western African religion emphasizing spirits and ancestor worship, which was brought by slaves to the New World.

INDEX

A

Aborigine (Australia) 6
Africa 4, 6, 8, 12, 13, 14,
   16, 18, 20, 22, 23, 24
Angola 14
Asia 10, 13, 14, 16, 24
Australia 6

B

Blumenbach, Johnann
   Friedrich 26, 27
Br'er Rabbit 22
Brother Rabbit 22

C

Carthage, Phoenicia 16
China 16
Clark, William 21

D

Democratic Republic of
   the Congo 14

E

Earth 6, 10, 14
Egypt 16
England 23
Europe 10, 13, 24

F

Finland 10

G

Ghana 18

H

Homo erectus 13
Homo sapiens 13

J

Jefferson, Thomas 21

K

Kentucky 21
Kenya 14

L

Lewis, Meriwether 21
Lewis and Clark
   Expedition 21
Linnaeus, Carl 24, 26

M

Madras, India 6
Mali 14, 18
Maori 6
Middle East 13, 16
Mississippi River 21

N

New World 22
New Zealand 6
Nigeria 14
North America 6, 20

P

Pacific Ocean 21
Philippines 6
Phillis 23

S

Sahara Desert 14, 16
Scotland 10
Senegal 23
Songhai 18
South Africa 14
Sweden 10

T

Tanzania 14
Tennessee 21

U

United States 20, 23, 28

W

Wheatley, John 23
Wheatley, Phillis 23
Wheatley, Susannah 23

Y

York 21